Dinosaurs

by Andrew Stephens

WATERBIRD BOOKS

Columbus, Ohio

 **Children's Publishing**

This edition published in the United States of America in 2004 by
Waterbird Books
an imprint of McGraw-Hill Children's Publishing,
a Division of The McGraw-Hill Companies
8787 Orion Place
Columbus, Ohio 43240-4027

www.MHkids.com

Library of Congress Cataloging-in-Publication Data is on file with the publisher.

First published in Great Britain in 2004 by ticktock Media Ltd.,
Unit 2 Orchard Business Centre, North Farm Road, Tunbridge Wells, Kent TN3 3XF.
Text and illustrations © 2004 ticktock Entertainment Ltd.
We would like to thank: Meme Ltd. Dinosaur illustrations by Pulsar Estudio.
Every effort has been made to trace the copyright holders, and we apologize in advance for any unintentional omissions.
We would be pleased to insert the appropriate acknowledgements in any subsequent edition of this publication.

Printed in China

1-57768-889-9

1 2 3 4 5 6 7 8 9 10 TTM 09 08 07 06 05 04

The *McGraw·Hill* Companies

Contents

Note to Parents and Teachers

The Busy Books series is designed to be both stimulating and accessible to young readers. Studies show that young children learn well through sharing. The activities in this book have been created with just that in mind. They provide an opportunity for you and your child to talk about the activities on each page. Stories, games, comprehension questions, and counting exercises offer a variety of ways to help your child learn new words, build basic skills, and practice letter and number recognition. Encourage your child to ask questions as you read together. By working with your child, you will be preparing him or her for the learning years ahead.

Dinosaurs:
Plant-eaters

Dinosaurs lived long ago before people were alive. Many dinosaurs ate only plants. They are called *herbivores*. The plant-eaters were the biggest of all the dinosaurs.

Ankylosaurus
(An-ky-lo-saw-rus)

This dinosaur had tough skin like a suit of **armor**. Even its eyelids were covered with a **strong**, bony covering.

Stegosaurus
(Steg-o-saw-rus)

This scary-looking dinosaur had **sharp spikes** on the end of its tail. Its brain was the size of a walnut.

Diplodocus
(Dip-lodo-cus)
This was the longest of all the dinosaurs. It had a long **neck** and **tail** and weighed as much as eight cars.

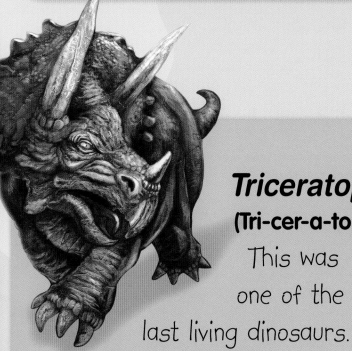

Triceratops
(Tri-cer-a-tops)
This was one of the last living dinosaurs. It used its big **horns** for fighting, like deer or rhinoceroses do now.

Dinosaur Words

Can you find these words on the page?

armor

spikes

neck

tail

strong

sharp

Dinosaurs:
Meat-eaters

Meat-eating dinosaurs are called *carnivores*.
Most meat-eaters walked on two legs. They had sharp teeth and claws to help them kill other animals. Some hunted in packs, while others hunted alone.

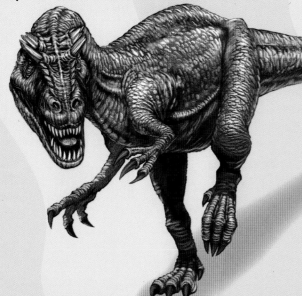

Allosaurus (Al-o-saw-rus)

This meat-eater had powerful legs and was a **fast** runner. It lived in what is now North America.

Giganotasaurus
(Jig-an-ot-a-saw-rus)

This was the **biggest** of all the meat-eaters. Its **long**, pointed **teeth** helped it chew its food.

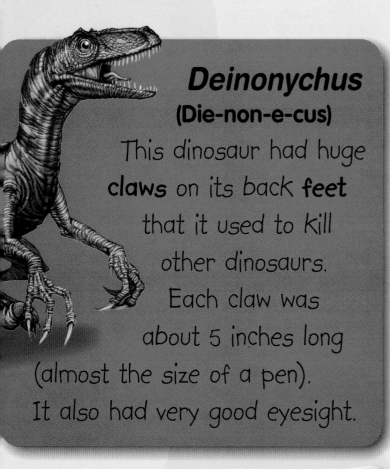

Deinonychus
(Die-non-e-cus)

This dinosaur had huge **claws** on its back **feet** that it used to kill other dinosaurs. Each claw was about 5 inches long (almost the size of a pen). It also had very good eyesight.

Velociraptor
(Vel-oss-e-rap-tor)

This dinosaur was much smaller than other meat-eaters. It was very **fierce** and hunted in **packs**.

Dinosaur Words

Can you find these words on the page?

fast

long

teeth

claws

fierce

packs

Word Puzzles

Look at these dinosaur pictures.
Can you put the words in the right order?

1

dinosaur

runs

fast

Dinosaur words

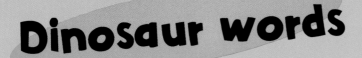

You have seen these words before. Use the pictures to help you say them.

spikes

teeth

8

sharp

are

teeth

2

hatching

The

eggs

3

tail

neck

claws

A Story to Read:
The New Arrivals

The mother dinosaur dug a **nest** using its giant claw.
Can you count the eggs it laid? One, two, three, and four!

It sat on the eggs to keep them warm until they began to move. With a crack, a pop, a squeak, and a yelp, four baby dinosaurs tumbled out.

The mother dinosaur searched for food among the trees. It found **grass, berries, leaves, and shrubs**. The babies would have plenty of food to eat.

Soon, the babies could walk and find food on their own. Now, it was time to leave the nest. They could join the dinosaur **herd**.

Can you answer these questions about the story you have just read?

1 Where did the mother dinosaur lay its eggs?
2 What did the babies eat?
3 Where did they go when they left the nest?

A Story to Share:
Stormy Hunting

Say the **boldface** words out loud.

The pteradon family lives high on a cliff. It is time for the mother to find fish to feed the hungry **babies**. Meanwhile, a bad storm is brewing.

Whooooosh! goes the wind as the dinosaur flies out to sea. It does not see any **fish** in the churning water below.

The storm is very strong! The dinosaur flies back to the **nest** to wait for the bad weather to pass. It is too late though! The mother pteradon is blown out to sea, far away from the nest.

Suddenly, the wind stops. The sea is calm again. It is full of fish that have also been blown out to sea. The mother pteradon eats a lot of fish to regain its strength. But which way is home?

With one last dive, the dinosaur gathers fish in its **beak** for the family. It flaps its strong wings and sets off for home.

The mother pteradon takes a moment to determine which way to go, but it is a long journey. Then, suddenly, the dinosaur sees its nest high on the cliff! The babies are very hungry now and gobble down the fish until they are full. What an adventure!

Dinosaur Hunt

Who will be the first dinosaur to reach the nest?

START

This exciting game is for 2 to 4 players!

First, find a small plastic toy for each player. Place each toy on the start line. Then, roll a die to see who goes first. The player who rolls the highest number goes first.

Take turns moving along the path, counting as you go. Follow the instructions on the rocks you land on. The first person to reach the nest wins.

9
Find dinosaur footprints. Move forward 3 spaces.

10

FINISH
Hooray! You're the first to reach the nest. You win!

18

1

2

3

4
Hide under a bush as an allosaurus runs past. Lose a turn.

7
See a herd of sleeping triceratopses. Go forward 5 spaces.

8

6

5

11

12

13

14
Fall into sinking sand. Lose a turn.

18

17
Find some ankylosaurus bones. Go forward 2 spaces.

16

15

A Bedtime Story:
Tilly's Lucky Escape

Like all young triceratopses, Tilly was always playing around. She could never remember to stay close to the herd.

Tilly was fascinated by all the plants and insects she could see. She watched an insect buzz from flower to flower as the sun went down. In the distance, the triceratops herd moved steadily further and further away.

Suddenly, Tilly noticed how quiet it was. She could not hear any of the sounds of the herd. Even at night, she could usually hear the sleeping dinosaurs breathing. But not tonight.

Tilly looked around her. It was empty now. Which way had the herd gone?

In the distance, Tilly could see a small forest. Triceratopses never went into the forest, but now the shelter of the trees looked more comforting than the empty grassland around her. Tilly set off for the trees. In the forest, hidden in the shadows, a huge tyrannosaurus rex watched Tilly coming closer and closer. It was not often that the T-rex found a triceratops on its own, especially such a young one. Although the tyrannosaurus was huge and had a mouth full of sharp teeth, it was scared of the three giant horns on the triceratops's head. But Tilly was young, and her horns were short.

Tilly saw the T-rex as soon as it stepped out of the shadow of the trees. Tilly began to bellow and stamp her feet to warn the tyrannosaurus. The T-rex stopped for a minute, but because Tilly was alone, it began to move forward again. Still bellowing loudly, Tilly lowered her head as she had seen the adults do.

The T-rex began to close in on Tilly. It was not looking around and was suddenly surprised when it was knocked onto its side. Struggling back onto its feet, the T-rex swung around to face a large, angry adult triceratops! Tilly's mother had arrived just in time!

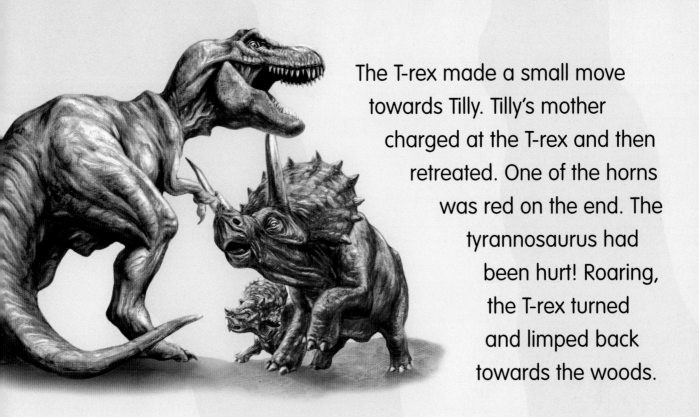

The T-rex made a small move towards Tilly. Tilly's mother charged at the T-rex and then retreated. One of the horns was red on the end. The tyrannosaurus had been hurt! Roaring, the T-rex turned and limped back towards the woods.

Tilly rushed to her mother's side. Then, the two triceratopses set off to rejoin the herd. Tilly was overjoyed to be reunited with the other dinosaurs. She had learned an important lesson—never again would she wander away from the herd!

Dinosaur Counting:
Dinosaur Line-up

How many dinosaurs are there in each line?

Can you count them?

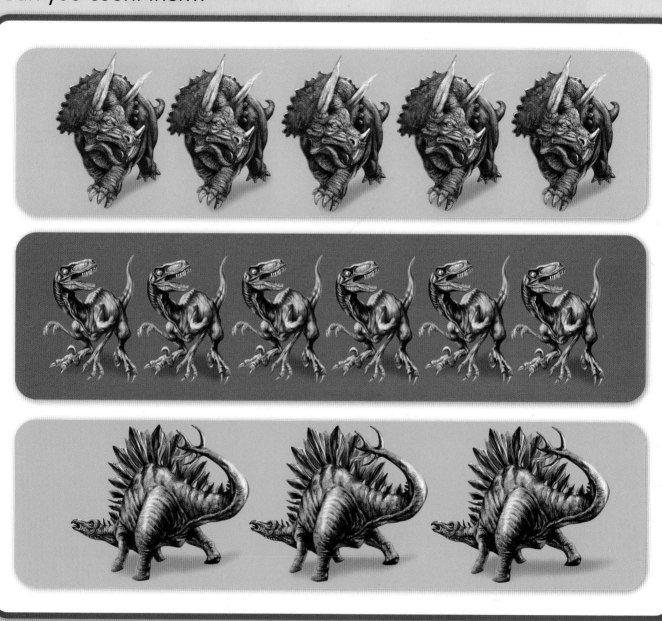

Which line has the most dinosaurs in it?

Which line has the least dinosaurs in it?

Can you match the number words to the right numbers of dinosaurs? Use the color codes to help you.

Number words

One Three Five

Two Four Six

Dinosaur Counting:
Dinosaur Babies

These two dinosaur mothers have laid some eggs.

How many eggs does dinosaur 1 have?

How many eggs does dinosaur 2 have?

Can you match these dinosaur mothers to their babies? Count the number of eggs to help you.

Which dinosaur has four babies? Which dinosaur has two babies?

Spot the Difference

Imagine if you could go on a dinosaur safari!

Look at these two pictures.
Can you spot the four differences between them?

Answers: 1. There is another baby on the bottom left. **2.** A red egg has been added in the back. **3.** The baby is missing from the egg in the front. **4.** The baby in the front is blue.

29

Make Your Own
Dinosaur Footprints

Did you know that in some parts of the world you can see actual dinosaur footprints?

You can make your own dinosaur footprints very easily.

You will need: 1. a big piece of paper 2. some large potatoes 3. paint and paintbrush 4. a saucer 5. an adult to cut the potatoes

1. Cut your potatoes in half (you will need an adult to do this for you.)

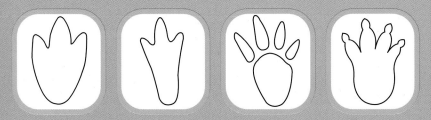

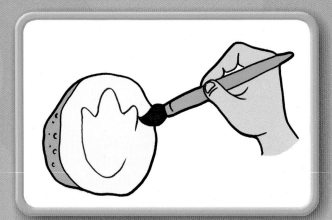

2. Paint a dinosaur footprint onto the flat side of your potato half. Use the examples above as a guide.

3. Get an adult to cut around the shape to make a raised footprint, like the one shown.

4. Pour some paint into a saucer. Then, dip your potato into the colored paint so the footprint is completely covered. Now you're ready to make dinosaur footprints!

5. Make your dinosaur trails on the paper. When you are making your prints, try to imagine how the dinosaurs would have walked. Look at the pictures below of how two- and four-legged dinosaurs walked.

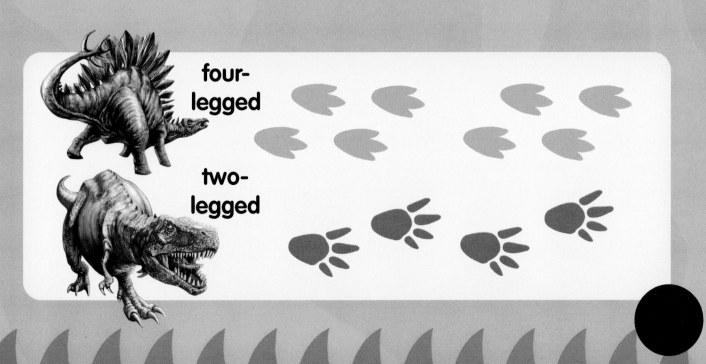

four-legged

two-legged

Word Finder

Here are some of the words used in this book. Can you remember what they mean? Go back and look through the book to see if you can find each word again.

herds	claws	packs
eggs	long	strong
teeth	berries	neck
tail	fish	sharp
nest	babies	feet
armor	fierce	hungry
spikes	horns	fast